MINECRAFT
GALAXY WARS

RISE OF THE STAR DEFENDERS

Book 1

BY HEROBRINE BOOKS

Episode 1

RISE OF THE STAR DEFENDERS

Dark times are upon us. Minecraft Mobs have taken over the galaxy under the sinister rule of Emperor Ender and Lord Nether. They have gained control of many planets across the solar system and developed vehicles and deadly weapons—none more devastating than the Death Cube that has the ability to destroy anything in its path.

The only hope for the universe lies with the Star Defenders—an elite group of kids who plan to restore peace to the galaxy…no matter the cost!

Chapter 1

DEFENDERS DISCOVERED

I felt my heart thumping in my chest as the Wither probes slowly approached across the vast dessert.

"There's about ten of them!" I called from the roof of our hideout as I gazed though my binoculars. "They're heading this way from the south."

Sky fastened down the metal hatches and we prepared for the onslaught. Ever since we left our home planet three weeks ago, we've been preparing for this moment. After all, now that the Minecraft Empire has control over most of our galaxy, we're no safer than anyone else. The only difference was that me and Sky weren't prepared to surrender.

Once she secured the last hatch, Sky joined me on the roof carrying her Blaster and handing me mine. I've known Sky all my life. Our parents had known one another since we were born just over fourteen years ago, and I never knew a world without her. I'd never tell her this, but she was like a twin sister to me. She was smart too—super smart. She had modified our spacecraft, DEFENDER 1, with sonic speed. This was the only reason we had managed to escape the invasion of our home planet and travel to this nearby moon undetected…until now!

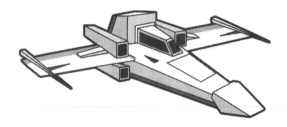

This was a barren place and there wasn't much here except us. It seemed that the Minecraft Empire were aware we had escaped and now sent these Wither probes to hunt us down and return us to the colony. Of course, we were having none of it! Sure, we needed to return home, but we were going on *our* terms.

"Is DEFENDER 1 ready?" I asked as Sky looked down the aim of her Blaster and got a Wither in her sights.

"That booster tube was one heck of a problem to fix, but I think I got it," Sky replied.

"You think?" I asked. "If that booster's not fixed, then we won't get far."

"You're gonna have to trust me, Ryan."

I hated it when Sky said that, yet she was always right. After all, she was one of the most gifted engineers in the universe. Not bad for a 14-year-old kid from a small colony in the outer reaches of the galaxy.

Sky's main problem was lack of patience.

"Now, are we gonna blast these Wither probes or keep wafflin'?" she joked.

I crouched beside her, took aim and ***fired!***

We shot one stream of green laser light after another from our Blasters. If the Wither probes weren't aware of our presence before, they certainly were now!

The Withers quickened their pace and the sand flew up around them in a storm.

"Maintain fire!" I cried, as both Sky and I continued to bombard the Withers with laser blasts.

MINECRAFT GALAXY WARS—BOOK 1

"**Yes!**" I cried, punching the air. "Got one!"

"Good work, genius!" Sky replied. "But it doesn't help if the other nine get through."

Sky flicked a switch on her modified Blaster, turning the laser blast from a single light into a broad beam.

"Watch this action, One Shot!" she called.

Sky stood up, stretched out her arm to full length and unleashed the fury!

Withers flashed and vanished before our eyes.

"Taken down like a clumsy clown!" Sky joked.

But the joke fell flat as a laser suddenly hit our hideout from above, sending rubble into the air around us and knocking us to the floor. I looked out at the Withers. There was only one left. I fired one last shot and missed.

"Come on!" Sky cried, grabbing my arm. "Let's get to DEFENDER 1 and get outta here."

As the craft above us continued to pound our hideout, we jumped into our spacecraft. It was a pretty clapped-out grey thing, but Sky being Sky had made some state of the art modifications.

"Hold on to your wig, Ryan!" she yelled, "and buckle up!"

We fastened our seatbelts, Sky pushed the central lever to full throttle and we blasted away from our hideout and into the sky.

"Those Wither probes weren't much bother," I said as we turned sharply above the desert moon.

"Nope! But they discovered where we were," Sky said. "Now quiet down so we can take care of this pest!"

We circled around and came up behind the thing that had attacked our hideout. It was one of Emperor Enders' Ender Dragons with a Zombie pilot on its back. The Zombie was armed with an Empire Gunner.

"Time to fly!" Sky whispered as she leveled off and **_fired!_**

The laser blast shot from our DEFENDER 1 craft and cannoned into the Ender Dragon. It flashed and vanished, causing the Zombie to squeal like a scared piglet as it plummeted to the ground.

"No need to fear when Sky is here!" Sky chanted, punching the air.

I had to admit, Sky was pretty awesome. Taking on the evil Minecraft Empire with her at my side would be a huge advantage. But we needed more recruits—two to be precise. I knew exactly who they would be, but finding them would be another matter!

Chapter 2

CREEPER TAVERN

We shot through space hoping that the sinister Minecraft Empire wouldn't detect us. It wasn't too far from the moon to our home planet so we had to develop a landing strategy fast.

"Okay! So we can't just rock up in the middle of town, can we?" I said.

Landing DEFENDER 1 there was not an option. Instead, we decided to land on the outskirts of our colony's settlement. We didn't want to be spotted, so once we were overhead, Sky put the craft into a steep descent until we swooped into a forest clearing and set the craft down.

I hit a button and the hatchway glided open.

Sky jumped out first, as she had to be the first to do everything, and took a look around DEFENDER 1. She put her hands on her hips and nodded. It seemed she was pretty happy with the speed modification she'd made.

"Lucky for you, I'm a genius!" she boasted. "If you were there on your own those Withers would'a had you for breakfast!"

I didn't need to reply. Sky and I got on great and I knew she was just joking around.

"Let's cover this thing up," I said, heaving some large fallen branches from the ground and hurling them over the craft.

"Hey, Ryan! Watch the paint work!" Sky threw some branches on too, a bit more delicately.

"Come on! Let's get into town quickly. We need to find Flynn and Ava and get out of here," I said, trying to be a bit more commanding.

Flynn and Ava were our other two best friends. We had known them for years. Flynn was the adventurous type who'd throw himself into anything, so I knew he'd be good in a fight against the Minecraft Empire. Ava was a bit of a joker and didn't take life too seriously. Still, she was loyal and I knew we could count on her.

The problem was that we didn't know their location. Sure, we knew they were in the town somewhere, but when the Minecraft Empire invaded and put the Enderman soldiers on patrol, Flynn and Ava vanished. Some feared they'd been taken away because they posed a rebellion threat. If I knew Flynn and Ava as well as I thought I did, I knew they'd be hiding out like we were and hatching a plan.

I grabbed two canvas sheets out of the back of DEFENDER 1 and threw one to Sky.

"Here! Put this over your head like a hood and cloak," I said. "The Enderman soldiers will be on the look out for us. We need to stay hidden."

Sky looked at the brown canvas sheet and gave it a smell. She recoiled. Yes, I have to admit, they smelled pretty bad, but it was our only choice. We threw them over our heads and ran into town.

The moment we got to the perimeter there were Enderman soldiers everywhere. This was going to be harder than I'd imagined. Just then, a Market Speeder carrying fruit to the town store pulled up next to us. As the pilot looked the other way to gain clearance from an Enderman, Sky and I jump on the back, unnoticed.

Within a minute, the Market Speeder was on its way. This would be perfect. The town store was right next to the tavern, and that was our best shot at learning where Flynn and Ava were hiding.

The tavern used to be a nice place to hang out with friends, but as we approached, I noticed the name on the sign above the door had been change to, *Creeper Tavern*.

That didn't sound good. As we jumped off the back of the Market Speeder and stomped towards the tavern entrance I was imaging only one thing inside—loads of Creepers!

I pushed the door open and led the way with Sky following. We pulled the canvas hoods closer to our faces as everyone looked in our direction. I glanced up slightly to see the room exactly as I had pictured it. The tavern was filled with Creepers. They were sitting at the bar and in the booths around the edge of the room. I could spot some old familiar faces amongst the crowd, but it was clear which Minecraft mobs were running this place now.

We went over to the bar and sat down. Luckily, the man who was serving the drinks was still the same. I had known him for a couple of years and he was a trustworthy source.

"Hi, Paul," I said, lowering my voice to not much more than a whisper. "This place has changed!"

"You're tellin' me!" Paul joked. "These Creepers are a nightmare and they don't pay for anything. What are you two doing back here?" Paul asked, glancing over at Sky. "I heard you'd escaped to the neighbor moon. You're crazy to come back."

"We need to find Flynn and Ava," I said, getting straight to the point. "Any word?"

Paul walked away and cleaned the inside of a few glasses with a towel. I could see he was looking over at an Enderman soldier in the corner of the tavern. He waited for the Enderman to turn away and then walked back over to us.

"The word is they're safe," Paul said and Sky and I let out a short sigh of relief. "I heard they've created a secret hideout just on the edge of town."

I leaned closer as a Creeper began to nudge me from the side.

"They're in the Robot Factory," Paul whispered. "That's all I know."

The moment Paul finished talking the Creeper knocked me clean off my stool. Normally I would have looked for an apology, but on this particular occasion I just wanted to get out of there. Some of the Creepers were beginning to look at us in a funny way and the Enderman soldier was now taking an interest too.

I flicked my head towards the door and Sky and I walked out of the tavern at the quickest pace possible without attracting more attention.

We had Flynn and Ava's location—the Robot Factory. All we had to do now was go and get them!

Chapter 3

ROBOT FACTORY HIDEOUT

Sky and I dashed across town as quickly as we could. I knew exactly where the Robot Factory was. It was a huge, silver warehouse-style building that you couldn't miss.

Inside, they made thousands of Homecare Robots. These were the types of robots that would clean your car, wash your windows, clean the dishes and scrub the toilets. However, if the Minecraft Empire had got their hands on the facility, I feared they'll be making something more sinister within those walls now!

There were several entrances and exits to the factory. I should know—I worked there for a couple of weeks during the holidays once and used every spare moment I could to escape outside and enjoy the sunshine. I knew one particular entrance that was tucked away and would allow us to gain access without being spotted.

I pulled the door open slowly, allowing a quick glance around the immediate factory floor to check for any guards. The coast seemed clear, so we sneaked inside and ran for cover behind a gigantic piece of machinery.

The noise in the factory was deafening. There were a hundred machines clanking and grinding and then there were about the same number of Zombie Pigmen working manually as well. They were standing at benches, punching rivets into sheets of metal and hammering out panels on robot body parts. The good thing was, with the factory being so noisy we didn't have to worry about tiptoeing around; we just had to stay out of view.

I looked along the production line at the finished robots. The ones we used to make were colorful and happy looking. These Minecraft Empire robots were black and silver and looked more like war machines than furniture polishers!

We scurried along the back wall behind the largest machines like a couple of rats. We stopped and looked around again. Where were Flynn and Ava? I had to think about if I were hiding out in here, where would I be?

It was then that I saw a square silver panel in the floor behind the next machine. I remember that it used to be a storage room years ago, but hadn't been used for some time.

I turned to Sky and gestured towards it. I grabbed the handle and pulled it open until it hinged up as high as my waist. The door locked in position and I ducked inside and down the stairs with Sky close behind me. The moment we were in, Sky pushed on the door and it closed tight—locking out nearly all the sound from the factory.

We stood on the stairs of the basement in complete darkness. Then, a single red laser beam flashed on below us. I could hear a Blaster charging. I had to speak now, before I got destroyed!

"Flynn? Ava? It's us! Ryan and Sky!"

There was a moment of silence. I didn't know what was going to happen. Then, the laser beam went dark and the lights flickered on.

Flynn and Ava were standing at the bottom of the stairs with their Blasters aimed in our direction.

"Okay, Trigger Twins!" Sky said, bounding down the rest of the stairs. "You can put those things away now."

She threw her arms around them both and I began to relax. It wasn't until then that I realized just how fast my heart had been beating!

"So, you coming down here or what?" Flynn chuckled.

I smiled and joined the other three. We had a massive group hug. It was good to see some friends again.

"So this is your palace?" I joked to Ava.

"Yeah, not bad, huh?" she replied, holding her arms out for me to have a look around.

To be honest, it was basic, but looked more comfortable that our temporary hideout on the neighbor moon.

It was pretty much a huge, underground square box. But one thing that immediately caught my eye was the spacecraft at the far end.

"What do you think?" Ava asked Sky as the tech genius wandered down to inspect it.

"Basic!" Sky replied, kicking a side panel. "But sturdy enough! I'll give it a few tweaks and that'll take it to the next level."

"How have you managed to build this thing?" I asked, puzzled by what an amazing job they'd done with no real way of getting any material to make it.

"It's all off cuts and rejected metal panels from the Robot Factory," Flynn said. "You see that rolling door over there?"

I looked past the spacecraft and could see a large door that obviously rolled into the ceiling.

"Just out the back is where they dump all the unwanted metal," Flynn continued. "All we have to do is wait for it to get dark and then we have the pick of the lot."

Sky didn't say much, but I could tell she was pretty impressed.

"How about you guys?" Ava asked. "Where's DEFENDER 1?"

"We had to land in the forest clearing on the other side of town," Sky replied. "It's chaos out there, you know."

"I can imagine," Ava sighed.

"Enderman guards everywhere," Sky continued. "I don't know how we made it through without being noticed.

"So, now we're together, what's the plan?" Flynn asked, pointing to a table and chairs in the corner.

We sat down and Ava poured out some water into a jug via a pipe they had tapped into near the rolling door. The water was slightly green. I gave it a sniff and politely declined!

"We have a plan to try and defeat the Minecraft Empire and restore peace to the galaxy," I said as the mood turned quite serious.

"Easier said than done!" Ava looked at Sky and me in disbelief.

"We need to get to the Death Cube," Sky chipped in. "That's the main base for the Minecraft Empire. We believe that both Emperor Ender and Lord Nether are there."

"Right, but you're not going to stand a chance of destroying that thing!" Flynn said. "It's the size of our planet!"

"No," I replied. "We need to get into the Death Cube and discover where they keep the Mind Crafter."

"What's a Mind Crafter?" Ava asked, as she leaned forwards.

"The Mind Crafter is the electric sphere that's at the centre of everything," I continued. "It's like a Minecraft mob brainwashing device. Whenever Emperor Ender or Lord Nether put their hands on it, it allows them to control the minds of Minecraft mobs everywhere."

"Assuming you find this Mind Crafter," Flynn said. "What then?"

"We have two choices," I replied. "We either steal it and use it to turn the Minecraft mobs from evil to good…"

"Or we destroy it!" Sky cried, thumping her fist on the table.

Just then, the lights flickered and went out. We sat in complete darkness and listened. Someone or something was trying to get in through the door in the ceiling.

"Quick, to DEFENDER 2!" cried Flynn.

"What's that?" I yelled as I got up form the table, not being able to see my hand in front of my face.

"That's what we've called out spacecraft over there," Ava replied.

"Original!" Sky commented sarcastically.

"No time for messing around, Sky!" I said as Flynn flicked on a flashlight. He rushed over to the roller door and pushed a button. The door groaned as it rose into the ceiling.

Ava jumped into DEFENDER 2 and fired it up.

The engines growled like a tiger. I had to be honest, the thing sounded awesome!

Flynn ran back and jumped in next to Ava.

I ran to the side of the spacecraft. "Just two seats?" I cried. "Great!"

"You two will have to make it back to DEFENDER 1," Ava shouted as the spacecraft hatch began to close. "Meet you on the far side of Spider Planet."

With that, they took off. I couldn't believe it. Nice rescue operation I was running here.

As DEFENDER 2 blasted away from the Robot Factory hideout, the metal door in the ceiling of the basement was forced open. The lights came on to full power and the sight that greeted my eyes terrified me to my very core.

Chapter 4

ENDERMAN PURSUIT

I froze on the spot as a group of Enderman soldiers came flooding down the stairs.

"How did they find us?" I cried.

"Must have been that Enderman in the Creeper Tavern. Doesn't matter now though!" Sky cried.

She was right. All that mattered at that moment was getting the heck out of there. I reached for my Blaster and Sky did the same. We stared at each other in a panic. We had both left our Blasters in DEFENDER 1.

The Endermen loomed towards us. We had no other option. Sky and I dropped our canvas disguises to the ground and ran.

We shot out of the huge doorway and into the scrap metal yard on the other side. There were fences on all four sides of us and towers of unwanted metal panels everywhere. Sky and I tried to climb up the stacked panels, but the edges of the metal were too sharp and I sliced my leg twice before giving up.

"Quick, stand between the two towers so there's no room for them to teleport next to you!" Sky shouted.

She ducked out of sight at one end of the scrap metal yard and I did the same where I was. It was then that I noticed the factories water tank above the roller door.

"What do you reckon?" I called to Sky. "Water kills Endermen, right?"

Sky looked at the tank and nodded.

I needed to think fast. The Enderman guards were halfway across the basement and getting faster. I pulled my sleeve down over my hand to stop the metal panels from slicing me and I pushed on the tower to my right.

The metal panels were piled as high as a house and began swaying from side to side.

"Push harder, dummy!" Sky shouted.

"I'm trying!"

I pushed again, and again, until the momentum toppled the tower of sharp-edged metal panels towards the factory. The first group of Enderman guards came hurtling into the yard as the panels fell onto the water tank, slicing it to pieces and sending a flood of water cascading down into the yard.

The Endermen flashed and disappeared. The remaining ones were trapped on the other side of the heap of metal and couldn't get out of the basement.

I ran to the factory wall and grabbed hold of one of the pipes that was hanging from the demolished water tank.

"Come on!" I called as Sky raced across the yard. "Up here!"

We climbed up the side of the factory as quickly as we could and leapt onto the flat roof. From there we could see across the town to the forest. We had to somehow get back to DEFENDER 1 and to our rendezvous point on Spider Planet. We'd lost Flynn and Ava once already since the Minecraft Empire invasion. I was determined that it wasn't going to happen again.

Sky and I ran across the roof and climbed into a tree on the other side. There seemed to be no mobs about, so we jumped down and headed for cover behind a fence.

We were both out of breath and rested with our hands on our knees for a few minutes to regain our strength.

When the time was right, we sneaked back though the town, keeping an eye out for Enderman soldiers who seemed to be patrolling the place looking for us. Somehow we made it. I wasn't sure if I should be relieved or paranoid. Had it been too easy?

Soon, we were at the far perimeter. We ran into the forest and jumped into DEFENDER 1. I closed hatch, Sky fired the engines and we blasted away from our home planet once more. I looked back and hoped that the next time I returned here, it would be free from the clutches of the Minecraft Empire.

For now, we had to set our course for Spider Planet to rejoin Flynn and Ava.

But, soon after we left the planet's atmosphere, I saw something heading towards us that made my blood run ice cold.

Chapter 5

ENDER DRAGON ATTACK

"Ender Dragon, dead ahead!" Sky cried, as she turned the defense shield to full strength.

I grabbed my control lever in my hands. Sky was controlling DEFENDER 1, but my controls had attack buttons built in, too. Together, we had to take this colossal, flying beast down.

It thundered towards us through space, its red eyes staring straight at us. It seemed that Lord Nether was aware we had evaded the Enderman guards and had sent his next line of defense to stop us.

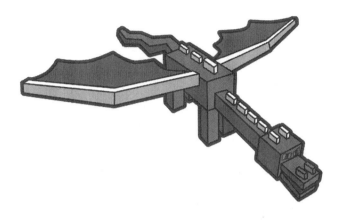

I was really scared. It had seemed like the Endermen were ordered to track us down and capture us. However, this Ender Dragon was on one mission only—to seek and destroy!

Sky turned DEFENDER 1 to the left. We were flying straight at it!

"Are you crazy!" I yelled. "If that thing hits us head on we'll be catapulted into the far reaches of space…or worse!"

"If we're going to get a shot off, we have to be facing it," Sky replied. "It's the only way."

She placed her thumbs over the red buttons on her control stick and I did the same. I clenched my fists tightly and fired!

Laser blasts shot from our craft and hurtled through space, smashing into the face of the Ender Dragon, causing it to turn to the side. Sky pulled the lever and thrust DEFENDER 1 into full throttle.

"Oh no, you don't!" Sky said. "You're not getting away from this pilot!"

But Sky pulled in too close and the colossal wing of the Ender Dragon came smashing down on our wing, sending us spinning into an involuntary roll. Sky managed to pull out of it and turn back, but the controls were hard to operate. We had lost thrust and the flap of the wing was completely smashed.

We had the beast in our sights once more. We fired again… **BOOM!** The Ender Dragon flashed violently and vanished.

I sat back in my seat as Sky punched the air with delight. But her celebration was cut short as DEFENDER 1 began to shake.

"Cut power to the left jet!" Sky shouted as she gripped the control lever and tried to steer the craft towards Spider Planet.

The Planet was right in front of us, but breaking through the atmosphere and landing with one engine in operation would be near impossible. Still, if anyone could do it, I knew Sky could. It was at that moment I was glad she was in control of DEFENDER 1 and not me.

Within a minute, we hit the planet's atmosphere and a burning red trail of heat shot out behind us. The craft shook uncontrollably. Sky pulled the lever to decrease the speed, but it wasn't as reactive as it should have been. We headed towards the dry, earthy ground. This was going to be a rough landing!

"Brace for impact!" Sky yelled as I pushed my hands onto the control panel in front of me. **"*Here we go!*"**

At the last minute, Sky pulled back on the lever and DEFENDER 1 crash-landed at full speed. We shot along the dry ground with a plume of brown dust filling the air and as the bottom of our craft scraped along the dry soil. We had no control. Luckily, there was nothing but barren earth all around us.

We gradually slowed and finally groaned to a stop.

"You okay?" I asked Sky, who seemed more shaken up than I was.

"Yeah!" she strained. "That was a close one!"

She popped the button on the cockpit and it automatically opened, letting in the intense, dry heat from outside.

"This place is a furnace!" Sky puffed, wiping her brow. "Why the heck did Flynn and Ava want to meet here?"

"I guess there's nothing here," I replied. "So we'll be safe while we develop our plan. The Minecraft Empire would have no reason to come to this planet."

But as those final words left my mouth, I realized that we were far from alone.

On the horizon was a collection of huts, and to the side of that it looked like a hole in the ground. I pulled out the electro-binoculars from under my seat and gazed through them in a panic. Exiting from the tunnel entrance was a mass of moving black objects, and they were scuttling quickly in our direction.

As I focused the binoculars I saw black creatures with eight legs and red devil eyes. As I suspected—Spiders were on their way.

Chapter 6

SPIDER PLANET

I realized that Spider Planet had its name for a reason! Those nasty hostile creatures must have seen our descent from space because they were on us faster than an ant on a grain of sugar!

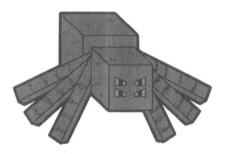

"Should be easy enough," Sky said calmly as she pulled out her Blaster and threw mine towards me. "Just think of it as a bit of basic target practice."

Sky went silent, took aim and ***fired***!

The first Spider she hit let out a nasty hiss, then flashed and vanished from sight.

"One down!" she yelled.

"Yeah! But there's like a hundred still to go!"

"So get shooting wise boy!" Sky smiled.

She was right. Standing by our craft and discussing the on-coming attack certainly wasn't helping.

I climbed onto the wing of DEFENDER 1, giving me a slightly better view of the Spiders. I fired up my Blaster and took them down.

One, two, three, four… I just kept striking one target after another. Sky was in her element too. Pretty soon, every Spider vanished. I jumped down from the wing and wiped my brow. For a few minutes I'd forgotten how hot Spider Planet was. It was almost unbearable.

"Come on!" said Sky, always keen to keep moving. "Let's head for that village on the horizon. Flynn and Ava can't have landed too far from here. We need to find them. Plus, we need to get some tools to fix our craft."

Sky began running towards the village before slowing to a quick stroll. I did the same. Running in that heat certainly wasn't a good idea.

It took us about an hour to reach the village. As we got closer I could see several nicely made huts and loads of Villagers. However, the Villagers were running around in a mad panic. Sky and I picked up the pace. As we got closer we saw Flynn and Ava hiding behind one of the huts and ran to their side as Villagers cried out in fear.

"What's going on?" I asked. "The Villagers seem terrified."

"It's the Creepers," Ava said. "The Minecraft Empire has sent them to destroy the Villagers of Spider Planet."

"I say we just crush them!" Flynn shouted, pounding his fist in his palm.

"With what, bird brain?" Ava said, tapping him on the head. "You try to destroy a Creeper with your bare hands and it'll finish you off."

"We've got our Blasters," I said, holding mine out in front of me.

"Ah! Perfect!" Flynn said, immediately swiping the Blaster from my hands.

He dived out from behind the hut and rolled across the ground in a completely unnecessary move that he must have seen in an action movie. Then, he let them have it!

He unleashed one blast after another at the Creepers as they turned and moved towards him. Many of the Creepers were hit and blew up in a second, but some dodged the onslaught. Meanwhile, in the center of the village, an Iron Golem was doing its best to protect the Villagers from the mass of green mobs. The big grey mob towered over the Creepers as the Villagers continued to hide in any place they could.

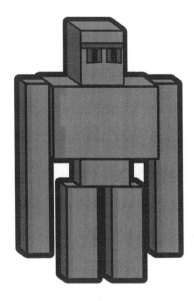

Suddenly, a Creeper was upon Flynn. It loomed towards him and knocked the Blaster from his hand.

It was clear Flynn needed some help, and it seemed that Sky was the one to provide it. She jumped out from behind the hut and blasted the Creeper at full power, as Flynn jumped for cover. The Creeper went up in an explosion, taking five other Creepers with him.

There were two Creepers left. They were attacking the giant Iron Golem. Sky darted towards them and unleashed tow final blasts. The Creepers blew up and vanished.

Sky leaned forwards and put her hands on her knees. Fighting Creepers in that heat was no easy task. She was worn out.

As Ava, Flynn and I walked across to her, the Iron Golem strode away and then came back with a glass of water and a poppy.

"What's the poppy for?" Sky said.

"The poppy is for you," the Iron Golem replied. "You saved us and you saved me."

"Oh! Err… thanks!" Sky replied, hesitantly taking the poppy. "It's just I'm… well, I'm not really a poppy kinda girl!"

"Just take the poppy and say thank you," I chirped in.

"Yeah, right! Thanks, giant grey guy!"

"I'm an Iron Golem," replied the Iron Golem.

"Of course you are," I said, trying to break into the conversation and bring it back to the important matter at hand. "We need to repair DEFENDER 1…"

"Who's DEFENDER 1?" the Iron Golem asked.

"It's not a who," I replied. "DEFENDER 1 is our spacecraft. We were just attacked by an Ender Dragon…"

As the name of that mob left my lips I could hear the entire group of Villagers gasp in shock.

"Don't worry," I continued. "The Ender Dragon won't be coming here. It was after us, not you."

The Villagers let out a collective sigh of relief.

"We can help," the Iron Golem said. "Where's your spacecraft now?"

I pointed to the horizon.

"Wait here," the mighty Iron Golem said. Then, it strode out to the horizon, picked up DEFENDER 1 as if it was made of cardboard and carried it back to the village.

The Villagers had a collection of tools and small metal objects and brought them out for Sky to look at. She picked out what she needed, tampered with the engine for a few minutes and then fired it up.

I have to say, she could have tested it in a better place. As the engines fired, they gave such a thrust that they knocked down three nearby huts!

We apologized, wished the Villagers and the Iron Golem safety on Spider Island and then prepared for takeoff.

Flynn and Ava ran to DEFENDER 2 on the other side of the village and together we blasted into the air, waved goodbye and shot back into space.

This time we set our course for the Death Cube. It was time to find Emperor Ender and Lord Nether and put a stop to their evil rule of the galaxy once and for all.

Chapter 7

APPROACHING THE DEATH CUBE

Once we were clear of Spider Planet, Sky hit the hyper lever and we shot into the depth of space leaving all planets and life behind us.

"What's the coordinates, Sky?" Flynn asked over the spacecraft radio. "Want to make sure we end up with you guys at the Death Cube and not in the middle of some asteroid storm near Planet 7."

"Coordinates for Lord Nether's lair is X76, Y35," Sky replied as she tampered with a few controls. "Should be coming out of hyper speed in less than three minutes."

I looked out through the cockpit. The stars blurred past us as we hurtled through space at more than thousand miles an hour.

If I was honest, I was getting nervous. None of us had ever seen the Death Cube. We had only heard about it from friends and whispers about the Minecraft Empire. It was supposed to be the mighty headquarters of the Empire, and it should have on it the object that Lord Ender used to control all the Minecraft mobs in the universe—the Mind Crafter. The legend says that whoever puts their hands on the Mind Crafter can control the mind of every mob in the entire galaxy. That was some power to have. It had fallen into the wrong hands for sure, and our mission was to find it and destroy it.

"Coming out of hyper speed," Sky said. "Brace for slow down."

Sky pulled back on the lever and I momentarily lurched forward in my seat as our speed decreased in an instant. We cruised past the stars at our usual speed. Then, in the distance we saw it.

"No way!" Ava said, over the radio. "It that it?"

No one replied. We were all in shock. Up ahead was the largest space block I had ever seen. It was the colossal grey space headquarters that the Empire had only recently constructed.

"So that's the Death Cube?" I said, in awe as much as in shock.

"Yep!" Sky replied. "Now everyone look lively. They've got Ender Dragons patrolling around it. Set cloaking device to max and keep your fingers crossed."

DEFENDER 1 shuddered as Sky activated the cloaking device. Everything looked the same to us, but on the outside we hoped we couldn't be seen. I looked over to DEFENDER 2… It was gone!

"We're still here!" Flynn laughed over the radio. "I assume you guys are there too. We can't see you!"

"Yeah! We're here," I said. "Good to know both our cloaking devices are working."

Suddenly, an Ender Dragon turned towards us.

"It's seen us!" I gasped.

"No chance!" Sky replied. "Not possible."

We watched the Ender Dragon closely. It moved towards us, then swooped to the right and turned away.

We continued towards the Death Cube and slowed our speed as we approached.

"Hey! Sky!" Ava said over the radio. "If the Ender Dragons can't see us, that's great, but if they don't know we're here, what will stop one from flying into us?"

It was a good question and not one any of us had the answer to!

"Well, we'll just have to hope they stay away," Sky said. "Still, keep on alert just in case. If one's on a collision course, we'll just have to move out the way."

The Death Cube began to loom over us as we approached. An Ender Dragon moved over the top of us, casting a dark shadow in the cockpit.

There was an entrance in the Death Cube wall. It looked like an abandoned hanger. We steered towards it and entered. The hanger was empty. We landed and powered down. We were inside the Death Cube. I took a deep breath. From that moment on, I knew the entire galaxy were counting on the four of us—four kids with a dream of peace and hope—four kids who went by the name of the Star Defenders!

Chapter 8

REACHING THE MASTER DOME

I hit the switch in front of me. The cloaking device turned off and the cockpit of DEFENDER 1 slowly hinged open.

Flynn and Ava did the same. We each slowly stepped from the spacecrafts and jumped down onto the floor. As our feet landed, it sent an eerie echo across the vast hanger.

"So, what do you think this hanger is used for then?" Flynn asked. "Seems like a waste of space."

"Huh! Like you!" Ava laughed.

"Shh! Keep it down, will you," Sky said, looking unusually annoyed. "If we get found out its game over. Not just for us, but for the entire galaxy."

"Wow! I suddenly feel a lot of pressure!" Ava joked.

"You should!" I added. "People are counting on us to do this."

Ava took a moment to think about it and then nodded her head.

"Here, take this!" Sky said, throwing her Blaster to Ava who was taken by surprise but managed to catch it anyway.

"We've got two Blasters. You guys take that one, Ryan and I can use his. We'll split into pairs. You two find the Power Hub and get this Death Cube shut down. With no power they'll be… err…"

"Powerless?" I added.

"Yeah! That's right," Sky continued, nudging me gently in the ribs.

"And what are you two gonna do?" Flynn asked, looking at me and Sky.

"I guess we're going to search for the Mind Crafter," I replied. "The only way to stop the Minecraft Empire from controlling the mobs is to destroy that transparent, deadly sphere."

We all seemed to know what we had to do. Flynn and Ava left the hanger first. There was no 'goodbye' and no 'good luck.' Just a nod of the head and they were gone. Part of me wondered if we would see each other again. Sky and I had known each other since we were kids and she obviously knew what I was thinking.

"Don't think like that," she said, putting her hand on my shoulder. "They know what they're doing. Now let's find that Mind Crafter and put and end to the Empire's rule once and for all."

Sky looked around and then darted across the hanger to a doorway on the other side. I gripped the Blaster firmly and followed.

We clung to the edges of the doorframe and look through into the corridor on the other side. It was like looking through the middle of a gigantic silver worm as it snaked away from us around a tight bend.

The coast seemed clear. There were no Enderman guards or Zombie commanders anywhere. Still, we moved on slowly. The Death Cube was a colossal place and I knew sooner or later we would encounter the enemy. For now though, the Minecraft Empire seemed unaware of our presence and the longer we kept it that way the better.

Sky signaled to me to move forwards. There was an elevator at the far end of the corridor, and we ran towards it quickly. However, just before we reached it, we heard footsteps.

We dived into a nearby storage room, leaving the door slightly open. I peered out. Huge Enderman guards were marching in our direction.

I pulled the door closed a little more, but could just about see what was going on. Four Endermen had marched to the elevator and were waiting to enter. They stood still, their eyes glowing pink as they starred at the doors. Then, with a **swish** the doors opened and the Endermen entered. Then after another **swish** the Endermen were gone.

"Come on!" I whispered, opening the door slowly and creeping over to the elevators with Sky behind me.

I pressed the elevator button and noticed my hands trembling.

"We'll be safe for a while once we get inside the elevator," Sky said. "I'll be able to reroute the circuit board so no one else can enter."

"Sounds good," I replied. "But what if someone's already in the elevator when it gets to this floor?"

It's obviously not something Sky had thought of and she took a moment to think about it.

"Well, then you blast them!"

Not the best plan, I thought. That would certainly be a great way to alert everybody that we were here.

Just then, I could hear the elevator stop. The doors hissed and slid open. Empty. Phew.

Quickly, Sky and I darted inside and closed the door. Sky immediately opened the circuit board panel and rewired the board to stop the doors from opening. I then hit the top button. Whispers around the galaxy said that Lord Nether controlled the Mind Crafter from a special glass dome on top of the Death Cube called the Master Dome. We were now traveling quickly to the highest level. If the Mind Crafter was there, we were determined to find it.

Chapter 9

THE MIND CRAFTER

The elevator stopped suddenly. We had reached the top. If our calculations were correct, when the doors opened we would be in the Master Dome—the central control hub for the entire Minecraft Empire.

I took a deep breath, readied the Blaster at my side and waited for the doors to slide back.

With a loud swish, the doors slid to the side. My eyes almost popped out of my head. We were standing on the edge of a huge glass dome. We stepped forwards. Above us was nothing but glass and the stars beyond. In the center of the room as a black podium, and sitting on it was a glass ball with bursts of lightning flashing around inside it.

"The Mind Crafter!" I said. Sky and I stepped towards it as the elevator doors slid shut behind us. "It's amazing!"

Suddenly, my body felt like it turned into stone as a sinister laugh echoed around the Master Dome.

"It certainly is!" came a voice from the shadows.

I turned and looked to the side. A huge dark chair slowly swung around. The figure sitting in it was Lord Nether.

He wore a black robe with a hood that obscured his face. All I could see beneath the hood were two red, glowing eyes.

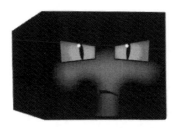

"It appears the mighty Star Defenders have finally found what they have been searching for," Lord Nether cackled as he rose from the seat and stepped slowly towards the Mind Crafter in the center of the dome. "This sphere is the source of all our power. With it we control the minds of every Minecraft mob in the galaxy."

I looked at Sky. I could feel my Blaster trembling in my hand. Lord Nether laughed.

"Look at you two!" he scoffed. "A little nervous are we? And to think you thought you could come here and destroy the Empire on your own."

Lord Nether moved towards a control console and pressed a button.

"Yes, Lord Nether," came a voice though a small speaker.

"Send four Enderman guards to the Master Dome. We have intruders."

Lord Nether released the button and walked over to the Mind Crafter. He closed his eyes and took a deep breath, then raised his black, gloved hands and placed them on the powerful sphere.

"The galaxy belongs to me and Emperor Ender, and there's nothing you puny kids can do to stop us."

Suddenly, the elevator doors slid open and four huge Endermen marched out.

"Seize those two," Lord Nether ordered, pointing his long, spindly finger at us.

I had heard enough. My hand was still shaking and my finger was twitching on the trigger of my Blaster. I raised it towards the advancing Endermen… and **fired**!

My first shot was a direct hit. It struck an Enderman, blasting it back against the wall before it flashed into a ball of light and disappeared. The other three looked less than pleased. They held out their long arms and lunged towards us.

"Sky! Look out!" I cried, as one tried to grab her.

Luckily, she was fast and dived across the floor, rolling behind a computer console for cover.

Lord Nether seemed completely unphased and remained calm with his hands placed firmly on the Mind Crafter.

I knew what I had to do. I crouched down, raised the Blaster with both hands and took aim at the glowing sphere of light. I pulled the trigger, but as I did an Enderman kicked the blaster from my sweating hands and sent it flying across the room.

I swung my leg in a wide sweep behind the huge dark mob, taking its legs from beneath it and sending it tumbling to the floor.

As it hit the ground, I jumped over it and ran to retrieve my Blaster. I turned and fired at the horizontal Enderman. It flashed and vanished. Two down, two to go!

Sky was doing her best to take down the Enderman guards too. She sprinted across to Lord Nether's desk and grabbed his personal Blaster that looked like it was made of pure gold. However, the second she touched it a wave of electricity flowed through her and she fell to the floor.

"Must be configured just for the evil Lord," I cried. "Leave it. I'll take care of these guards."

I unleashed a series of blasts that took the final two Enderman guards out. They flashed and disappeared.

"Well, well," chuckled Lord Nether. "You two have done better than I expected. Congratulations!"

"It's time to end this, Lord Nether," I said, brandishing my Blaster in front of me and stepping carefully towards the evil Minecraft lord. "The galaxy isn't yours to control. Now, step aside and let me destroy that Mind Crafter."

"Oh, dear," Lord Nether said with a rye smile. "Someone is getting a bit too confident, aren't they?"

He slowly lifted his spindly, gloved hands from the electrical sphere and turned to face me. He held out his arms like some sort of zombie and pointed his fingers in my direction. Then, it hit me. He unleashed a colossal bolt of lightning. It shot from the tips of his evil fingers and struck me in the chest. It felt like a magnet as it pulled me slowly towards him. He raised his hands slightly and I lifted into the air. My chest felt tight, as if a huge rubber band was wrapped around me and getting tighter by the second. I dropped my Blaster. The pain was getting unbearable.

Then, with a deadly look in his eyes, Lord Nether shot his fingers out as straight as they would go and I hurtled back against the wall. I smashed into it at full force and dropped to the floor as he released his electrical energy from me.

"*Ryan!*" Sky called as she raced across from Lord Nether's desk towards me. But, she was not safe either. As she headed in my direction, Lord Nether flicked his fingers and a small bolt of lightning shot from his finger tips and knocked her to the floor.

The elevator door beside me was open. I looked at the Mind Crafter and then at Sky. She was in pain too. We had no choice but to retreat.

As Lord Nether returned his hands to the Mind Crater and closed his eyes, Sky and I got to our feet and hobbled into the elevator. As the door closed and we descended back into the depths of the Death Cube I felt our chance to save the galaxy had slipped through our fingers. And things were about to get worse.

As the elevator descended Sky opened a small circuit board hatchway near the door. She hacked into the main security system to see if Flynn and Ava had managed to power down any of the Death Cube systems. As she scanned the security files it was clear that all the systems were still in place. But that wasn't the worst news. She plugged into the prison block system. Our worst fear had come true. Flynn and Ava had been captured.

Sky programmed the elevator to stop at sub level 12. We had to get to the prison block and rescue our friends.

Chapter 10

THE PRISON BLOCK

The moment the door opened in the prison block we leapt into the corridor and headed for the cells. The corridor was darker and narrower in this part of the Death Cube. I felt uneasy. There were no Enderman guards about, yet surely they must be expecting us?

Soon, we reached the end of the corridor. There was nothing in front of us except for a fortified blast door. There was an access button on the side. Sky leaned forwards tentatively and pressed it.

Suddenly, the door slid open and laser fired descended on us like nothing I had seen before. We ran into the room and dived behind a couple of pillars for cover as the lasers zipped past us.

The blast door slid shut. Whatever battle lay ahead, we had no choice but to confront it.

"Good work genius!" Sky said, unarmed and helpless to do anything. "You seem to have gotten us locked in the main prison block. What's the plan now?"

"We need to find the cell that's holding Flynn and Ava. We have to get then free and then get off this Death Cube. Our plan isn't going as well as it was supposed to. We have to regroup."

The lasers continued to hurtle past us. I decided I had to peer around the pillar and work out how to take down our attackers. I took a deep breath, readied my Blaster and glanced around the pillar as quickly as could.

"There's no one there," I cried as I took cover behind the pillar once more.

"What are you talking about?" Sky replied. "Then where are those laser blasts coming from?"

"They're automatic laser blasters," I replied.
"They're coming from wall mounted attack
modules. There are no Enderman guys in sight!"

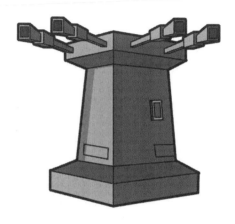

I gripped my blaster tightly in my hands, took a
deep breath and jumped out from behind the
pillar. I took aim at the first wall mounted laser
blaster I could see. I struck a direct hit and the
machine exploded in a ball of flames.

Suddenly, another blaster struck my shoulder
and I spun to destroy that one too. I kept going,
jumping from side to side to try and evade the
lasers.

Another one hit me in the shin and I destroyed it with a single blast. The laser blasts were subsiding. There was just one wall mounted machine left.

I ran forwards and ducked behind a computer console. I took a moment to regain my breath. Then, I jumped up, took aim and destroyed the machine. **BOOM!** It exploded in a small ball of flames and the onslaught of lasers stopped.

I dropped to the floor. I was out of breath. Sky ran towards me and took the heavy Blaster from my hands.

"You okay, Ryan?"

"Just about," I replied. "Go and hack into the computer and find out which cell Flynn and Ava are held in. Let's get them and get them outta here."

Sky stood up and started hacking into the main security system. I remained on the floor as my breathing returned to normal. I held my shoulder and then my leg. The lasers had caused some serious bruising, but luckily they had inflicted no more damage than that.

Finally, I managed to pull myself to my feet and take back the Blaster from Sky.

"Seems like there aren't many prisoners in here," she said, scanning the system.

"I guess no one else is crazy enough to try and break into the Death Cube," I joked.

"Here we go. They are being held in cell 253 and 254."

A long corridor ran directly away from the security room. We moved down it as quickly as we could until we reached the two cells we were searching for. I hit the access button on one as Sky did the same on the other. The doors slid open and our prisoner friends were revealed.

"*Ryan? Sky? Wow!* Are we glad to see you!" Ava said as we all hugged. "Did you destroy the Mind Crafter?"

"Almost," I replied. "But Lord Nether was in the Master Dome. He has powers beyond ours. We had no chance."

"What happened to you guys?" Sky asked. "Did you manage to power down any of the Death Cube systems?"

"We never had a chance," Flynn replied. "We were captured pretty quickly. We must have only been away from DEFENDER 2 for a few minutes before Enderman guards swooped on us and dragged us up here."

"Talking about DEFENDER 2," I said. "We should get back to our spaceships."

Suddenly, the dim lights in the prison block turned to red and an alarm rang out.

"Sounds like they're onto us again," Sky said.

"Let's get out of here," I ordered, taking a tight grip of my Blaster. "We should regroup on a far away planet and form a new plan."

The others were in complete agreement. We headed quickly from the prison block and ran through the maze of corridors back to our spaceships. Once inside DEFENDER 1, Sky hit the main throttle and we blasted from the Death Cube with Flynn and Ava beside us in DEFENDER 2. However, as we shot back into space we quickly realized we weren't alone.

"Attackers in hot pursuit!" Sky shouted over the radio.

"What are they?" I cried, struggling to see out the back of the cockpit.

"Enderman Space Pods," Sky replied.

It appeared we weren't safe yet!

Chapter 11

THE CHASE

"**S**witch on deflector shield and brace for impact," Sky called as a faint purple bubble appeared around our spacecraft.

I looked across to DEFENDER 2. Flynn and Ava had done the same. The deflector shield wouldn't keep us completely safe, but it would stop us being blasted from space for a short time.

Then, as we hurtled away from the Death Cube at 200 mph, the onslaught began.

The Enderman Space Pods moved into formation and began their attack.

There were four of them and they rose above us, one behind the other before diving at full speed. Then, they unleashed their lasers.

They rocketed into us, shaking DEFENDER 1 as if we were in the middle of an earthquake. Luckily, DEFENDER 2 was on the case.

Flynn and Ava looped up higher and destroyed the leading Enderman Space Pod. It exploded in a colossal ball of flames, shaking us more than the laser blasts had done.

The second Enderman Space Pod ploughed into the first and was destroyed as well.

"Awesome shot, Ava!" I shouted over the radio. "I think you just saved us."

"Glad to return the favor," she replied.

The remaining Enderman Space Pods split up and swerved round onto our tail.

"Got one directly behind us," Sky shouted.

"Us too!" cried Flynn. "What's the plan now?"

Luckily, Sky was an incredible pilot and knew exactly what to do. She flew down in front of DEFENDER 2 with the Enderman Space Pod still behind us. This now meant that we were in the lead with an enemy Space Pod behind us, then DEFENDER 2 behind them, followed by the last Enderman Space Pod.

"Blast the pod behind us," Sky said to Ava over the radio.

Ava didn't hesitate. She hit the red button on her control lever and unleashed a single blast at our pursuing Space Pod. It exploded, meaning all that was left now was us, followed by DEFENDER 2 and then the last remaining Enderman Space Pod at the back.

"Glad we saved you," Flynn cried, "but who's going to save us?"

"Leave that to me!" Sky replied.

She gripped the control lever with both hands and pulled it sharply backwards. DEFENDER 1 shot vertically into the air and I was pushed back into my seat with the force. Then, we moved upside-down. Sky was performing a loop-the-loop.

"Almost there!" she radioed to DEFENDER 2 as Flynn and Ava came under fire.

Then, with one final maneuver, Sky brought our spacecraft down directly behind the final Enderman Space Pod and fired.

BOOM!

The enemy was defeated.

As we turned to head to the nearest planet of Iceatope we flew over the top of the Death Cube. Lord Nether was still inside with his hands on the Mind Crafter. I knew there and then exactly what we had to do.

"We need to take out that Mind Crafter," I said to Sky, leaning forwards and placing my hand on her shoulder. "Lord Nether is still in there. If we destroy the Mind Crafter and him as well, we can bring peace to the galaxy."

"Affirmative, Ryan!" Sky replied, giving me a thumbs-up. "That was exactly what I was thinking."

We radioed the plan to DEFENDER 2 and flew down under the Death Cube to ready ourselves for the attack. But, before we could level off a colossal hatch opened underneath the Death Cube. My blood ran cold. Out from the hatchway flew an army of Ender Dragons!

Chapter 12

ENDER DRAGON ATTACK!

The Ender Dragons swarmed out of the Death Cube and quickly built up speed.

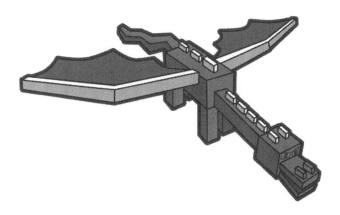

We flew up the side of the Death Cube and over the Master Dome at the top. Lord Nether was inside and clearly controlling the deadly flying beasts.

We opened fire on the huge glass dome, but the shots just bounced off the surface and didn't even cause Lord Nether to look up. We flew around for another attempt as DEFENDER 2 flew alongside us.

"Let's try again," I said over the radio. "Except this time you shoot at exactly the same time as us. Maybe hitting with double the power will destroy the dome."

But, before we could put our plan into action we had a more immediate problem. I glanced to my left. A colossal Ender Dragon was heading straight for us. I clenched every muscle in my body and braced for impact.

SMASH!

With the force of a speeding freight train, the giant beast struck the side of DEFENDER 1, catapulting us away from the Death Cube and sending us into an intense downward spiral.

"I can't control it!" Sky shouted, gripping the control lever with all her strength.

"Come on Sky!" I cried. "Pull us outta this!"

I was staring to go faint. We were in a spin and seemed to be getting faster by the second. Several miles below us was the frozen planet of Iceatope and we were heading straight for its surface.

I could hear Sky groaning to grip the lever even harder and pull us out of the descent. With one final attempt, she seemed to do it.

The spinning decreased and we gradually began to flatten to a horizontal flight. Sky had done it, but she was completely drained.

"Sorry, Ryan!" she huffed as she tried to regain her breath. "That was closer that I would have hoped. Where's Flynn and Ava?"

We looked up through the top of the cockpit. DEFENDER 2 was hurtling around the Death

Cube, being pursued by the pack of Ender Dragons.

"Looks like those guys need our help!" I cried.

Sky agreed. She pointed DEFENDER 1 up at the Death Cube and we shot away from the planet's surface.

"Come in DEFENDER 2," I said over the radio. "We're on our way."

"Better sped it up, Ryan," Ava replied. "The Ender Dragons are playing dirty!"

We flew up behind DEFENDER 2 and blasted four Ender Dragons. Each was a direct hit and caused them to flicker and vanish. There were four left.

"Let's split up," Sky said. "Flynn, you take two and leave the other two for us."

DEFENDER 2 banked to the right and two of the huge beasts followed. As they turned away, Sky fired a flurry of lasers, and after two attempts, struck both dragons with direct hits. They disappeared. Only two remained.

Suddenly, Sky banked and headed straight towards the Death Cube wall. She picked up speed.

"What are you doing?" I asked. "You're flying straight at the Death Cube!"

"No kidding, Captain Obvious!" she yelled.

"Okay. Care to explain why?!"

Sky didn't respond. She moved the lever slightly to the side and propelled DEFENDER 1 towards a series of jagged pieces of metal on the Death Cube's surface.

I covered my eyes and braced for impact. "We're gonna hit!" I screamed.

"Not today!" Sky shouted.

She pulled back on the control lever and the spacecraft shot vertically up the Death Cube wall, causing both pursuing Ender Dragons to slam into the sharp pieces of metal and disappear from sight.

Sky swung away and celebrated with a victory roll.

DEFENDER 2 rocket out of nowhere and flew beside us.

I looked over at the Master Dome. Lord Nether was inside and must have been fearing for his safety. He placed his hands under the Mind Crafter and carefully lifted it from the podium. He glanced our way. I knew that if we were going to destroy the Mind Crafter and Lord Nether, it had to be now.

I hit the co-pilot button, took over the controls from Sky and thrust DEFENDER 1 higher into space. We shot up and up until the Death Cube became a dot beneath us. Then I looped through the air and shot back down towards the Master Dome at full speed.

Lord Nether was going to get away. I felt a wave of determination wash over me. I squinted. I had the Mind Crafter in my sights. I hovered my thumb over the blaster button and prepared to fire.

Chapter 13

KA-BOOM!

I shot towards the Master Dome on top of the Death Cube. Lord Nether was inside. He was carrying the Mind Crafter and was almost at the elevator door. But, to my surprise, he didn't go into the elevator. He ran through a door beside it. I couldn't worry about where he'd gone. I just knew that if I destroyed the Death Cube then there was no way Lord Nether and that Mind Crafter would survive.

The Death Cube was upon us. The Master Dome was dead ahead. I threw my thumb onto the button and *fired!*

DEFENDER 2 approached beside me and did the same thing at exactly the same time. Our combined shots formed a mega laser. It hit the glass and sent a crack ripping through the center of it as smoke started flooding from within.

Suddenly, a small pod shot out from beside the Master Dome. Lord Nether was inside. He was escaping.

I pulled on the lever to turn DEFENDER 1 around, but Sky took control.

"We need to get Lord Nether!" I cried.

"We need to save our lives!" Sky replied.

I punched the back of her seat in frustration as she locked me out of the control system and turned DEFENDER 1 towards Iceatope. She hit full power. DEFENDER 2 flew beside us. Suddenly, the Death Cube rumbled, shook and exploded in a giant ball of flames.

"KKKKAAAABBBBBOOOOMMMM!!!!

The explosion rocketed us towards the ice planet at a mammoth speed. As it died down, Sky eased back on the controls and prepared to land.

I looked back out to space. The Death Cube was gone and Lord Nether was nowhere to be seen.

"Reckon we blew him away as well!" Flynn shouted over the radio.

I looked out of the cockpit and across to the cockpit of DEFENDER 2 as Flynn gave Ava a high five.

"Don't be so sure," I replied. "If he got away with the Mind Crafter then the galaxy is no safer than it was before."

"Well, how will we know?" Sky chipped in as she slowed DEFENDER 1 to walking pace and then placed us safely on the surface of Iceatope.

I hit the cockpit button and it eased open.

I looked around. The surface of Iceatope was freezing. "I guess we'll only know when we come across another mob. If it behaves in its usual way then I guess old Nether and the Mind Crafter have been destroyed."

"Oh, yeah!" Flynn cried with a huge smile on his face.

"But if the mobs are still under his control then they will be more hostile than ever and ready to capture us," I continued.

I looked around the cockpit area for some thicker clothes before we all froze to death. There was nothing available.

My teeth were beginning to chatter and I wasn't the only one feeling the intense cold. I could see that Ava was shivering from head to toe.

"What's that over there?" Sky said, pointing so some sort of lone building standing in the middle of a vast plain of snow.

I grabbed the binoculars from beside my seat and looked into the distance.

At first the view was blurry. I adjusted the settings.

"Looks like a small hut." I replied. "And there's smoke coming from a chimney."

"F-f-fire," said Flynn, his teeth beginning to chatter too. "Th-th-that m-m-means w-warmth."

Flynn was right. We climbed out of the cockpits of our spacecraft and began the slow walk through the thick snow towards the hut.

As we approached I heard several creatures clattering around inside. I raised my hand and knocked on the door. We stood motionless, shivering in the freezing temperature. Then, the door opened.

I gasped and my lungs froze as the cold air rushed into them. Standing before us were two Enderman guards. Their eyes were glowing, and they had handcuffs at the ready.

They slapped the handcuffs around our wrists before we had time to react. We were caught. Lord Nether must still have the Mind Crafter. His grip on the galaxy was still intact. Our mission for the Star Defenders to save the universe seemed at an end.

Suddenly, the cold became too much. I felt my heart rate slow. My eyelids dropped, shutting out all daylight. I must have fainted, because the next thing I knew I was locked in a tiny, concrete prison cell. I was all alone. My life was over. The Minecraft Empire had won.

FIND OUT WHAT HAPPENS NEXT IN...

Minecraft Galaxy Wars–Book 2
"Hunt for the Hidden Empire"

Coming Soon...

If you really liked this book,
please tell a friend right now.
I'm sure they will be happy you
told them about it.

PLEASE LEAVE US A REVIEW

Please support us by leaving a
review on Amazon. The more
reviews we get the more books
we will write!

CHECK OUT OUR OTHER BOOKS FROM HEROBRINE PUBLISHING

The Diary of a Minecraft Zombie Entire Book Series

Get The Entire Series on Amazon Today!

The Mobbit:

An Unexpected Minecraft Journey

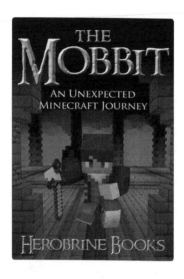

Get The Entire Series on Amazon Today!

The Ultimate Minecraft Comic Book Series

Get The Entire Series on Amazon Today!

Steve Potter and the Endermen's Stone

Get The Entire Series on Amazon Today!

Herobrine Goes To School

Get The Entire Series on Amazon Today!

An Interview with a Minecraft Mob

Get The Entire Series on Amazon Today!

Ultimate Minecraft Secrets:
*Minecraft Tips, Tricks and Hints
to Help You Master Minecraft*

Get Your Copy on Amazon Today!

The Ultimate Minecrafter's Survival Handbook:

Over 200 Tips, Tricks and Hints to Help you Become a Minecraft Pro

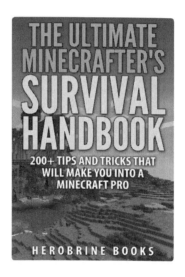

Get Your Copy on Amazon Today!